Become the Hero of Your Own Story

52 Tips to Teach Today's Teens

Elysia Butler

Become the Hero of Your Own Story
52 Tips to Teach Today's Teens

Copyright © 2022 by Elysia Butler

The Daily Compass, Inc.

ISBN 979-8-9859778-0-6 (paperback)
ISBN 979-8-9859778-1-3 (hardcover)

Printed in the United States of America.

NOTE FROM THE AUTHOR

Being a teenager today is more challenging than it's ever been before, but it is possible for teens to rise above the challenges and become the hero of their own stories.

To the teenagers reading this, I love you; and I know that you are capable of more than you think. Be kinder and gentler with yourself. Life can be challenging, but you are one incredible person. You have a story to tell, so find the strength you need. Take the adventure on, learn the lessons, and rise above. Know that you are enough. I believe in you.

To the parents reading this, remember to be positive, nonjudgmental, and have open conversations beginning with love and light as you travel through the modern-day monsters your teens are facing today. I invite you to be patient and remember that you don't have to know, nor will you know, all the answers to everything that is happening in your teenager's life...and that's okay. You are not alone.

I believe it is time for teens and parents to rise together in becoming the hero of their own stories.

Please reach out to share how you are implementing "The Hero's Journey" in your day-to-day life, with your family and friends, and in all your adventures.

I would love to hear about the success you have with incorporating these tips and have further discussions about your journey.

Xo, Elysia Butler

Website–www.thehopehero.com
Mentorship Options–Self Study, Group Coaching, and Individual Programs
Instagram–@risewithelysia @thehopehero
Facebook–Elysia Butler
TikTok–@iamahopehero
Email–risewithelysia@gmail.com

HOW TO USE THIS BOOK

This calendar has been inspired by the teens in my classroom over the last 14+ years. The quotes of inspiration I put on my board each week have influenced the contents of this book. The life lessons I engage my students in are part of my classroom philosophy and help to navigate teens through Joseph Campbell's "The Hero's Journey," while connecting the applications for life today.

Fun Fact: After many years in the classroom teaching English, I have found that teenagers rarely capitalize and punctuate correctly. So, as a special feature, I have purposely not capitalized the beginning of sentences, names, and left every "i" lowercase. As well, I have deliberately omitted many periods and commas throughout the book.

The intention of this guide is for teens and parents to travel the stages of "The Hero's Journey" throughout the year to inspire hope for a brighter future, gain confidence, and overcome whatever trials are placed before them.

Flip through the pages week by week to discover a tool and life lesson to talk about with your teenager. On the backside, there is a quote to connect to the messages. I believe every teenager needs to hear these words from an adult who loves them.

Too many teens today are struggling with anxiety, depression, and suicidal thoughts that consume their lives and the lives of those around them. My intention for you is that this guide will bring a shimmer of hope, resiliency, and purpose into your home and the lives of your family members.

I am grateful for the incredible opportunity to work with teens today and be part of this chapter in their adventure.

I cannot wait to hear about the success you have with incorporating the tips on the following pages for becoming the hero of your own story.

DEDICATION

This book is dedicated to Douglas Cannon, my father, and my everyday hero.

As the youngest and only girl in my family, my relationship with my dad holds a sacred place in my heart.

My father was a true American hero who served valiantly in the Vietnam War, received a Purple Heart for his courageous perseverance, and continued to be a soldier for good throughout his life.

My dad served his whole career as an educator and principal in Davis School District for 34 years.

On Veteran's Day, November 11, 2021, my father unexpectedly passed away while teaching students in my classroom. Some of his last words were about his love for our country and his gratitude for all those who continue to fight for our freedoms today. One of the last stories he told was how he met my mom, "the love of his life."

My father lived every day as his own hero, an American hero, and a hero to all those who had the privilege of knowing him as the incredible man he was.

Dad, I miss you every single day.

Thank you for being the hero of your own story and the hero who taught me the way to live, love, and serve all those who I meet on my own hero's journey.

I love you always!

SURROUND YOURSELF WITH PEOPLE WHO HELP YOU TO BE THE BEST VERSION OF YOURSELF

"you are the average of the 5 people you spend the most time with"
—Jim Rohn

YOU ARE A REFLECTION OF THOSE YOU SPEND TIME
WITH & THEY ARE A REFLECTION OF YOU

IF THOSE YOU'RE SPENDING TIME WITH ARE NOT "FUN" ANYMORE

OR IF YOU DON'T FEEL GOOD ABOUT YOURSELF
AFTER SPENDING TIME WITH THEM

THEN IT'S TIME TO MAKE A CHANGE

MAKE SURE THAT WHEN YOU SAY "YES" TO SOMEONE ELSE

YOU AREN'T SAYING "NO" TO WHAT IS RIGHT FOR YOU

IT'S OKAY TO CHOOSE A DIFFERENT
PLAYGROUND (OR FRIEND GROUP)

FAIL FORWARD EVERY STEP OF THE WAY

"fail early, fail often, but always fail forward"
-john c. maxwell

THERE IS NO SUCH THING AS PERFECTION

FAILING & FALLING DOWN IS A NORMAL PART OF LIFE

IT'S OKAY TO FALL, BUT MAKE SURE YOU KEEP GETTING UP

IF YOU NEED HELP FIGURING OUT HOW TO GET BACK UP, ASK

FAILURE CAN BE THE GREATEST TEACHER IN YOUR LIFE

LEARN THE LESSON & RISE AGAIN

EVERYONE YOU ADMIRE HAS FALLEN DOWN MANY TIMES...

YOU JUST DON'T KNOW THEIR STORY YET, SO ASK THEM

YOUR FEAR KEEPS YOU FROM BECOMING THE BEST VERSION OF YOURSELF

"the cave you fear to enter holds the treasure you seek"
—joseph campbell

THE FEAR WE CREATE IN OUR IMAGINATION IS SCARIER THAN THE ACTUAL DOING OF THE TASK WE'VE BEEN AFRAID TO DO

ENTER THE "CAVE:

LEARN AS YOU GO

FIND TOOLS & MENTORS

CREATE FRIENDSHIPS TO HELP YOU ALONG THE WAY

YOU WILL FACE MANY "MONSTERS" IN YOUR MIND

PUSH PAST THE DOUBTS & CONTINUE

DON'T LET FEAR KEEP YOU FROM LEARNING THE LESSONS THAT LIFE HAS TO OFFER

THE TREASURES & GIFTS ARE WAITING FOR YOU

DAILY DECISIONS CREATE HABITS FOR YOUR FUTURE

"two Roads diverged in a wood, & i—i took the one less traveled by, & that has made all the difference"
—Robert Frost

THERE ARE MANY ROADS YOU WILL TRAVEL IN LIFE

CHOOSE YOUR PATH

NAVIGATE YOUR DECISIONS

KNOW THAT YOU WILL MAKE MISTAKES
& THAT'S PART OF THE JOURNEY

IT'S OKAY TO HAVE A DIFFERENT PATH THAN OTHERS

HAVE FUN & LIVE YOUR LIFE ON PURPOSE

"ife is a game, play it"
—mother teresa

STOP WAITING FOR ADVENTURE & HAPPINESS TO FIND YOU

GO & MAKE THOSE MOMENTS

BE PART OF SOMETHING, INVITE YOURSELF & CREATE IT

TAKE EVERY OPPORTUNITY TO PLAY & HAVE AN INCREDIBLE TIME

SCHEDULE THINGS THAT MAKE YOU HAPPY EVERY SINGLE DAY

LET GO OF HOW YOU THINK LIFE SHOULD LOOK

LAUGH OUT LOUD, DANCE AWKWARDLY, TAKE THE CHANCE

PLAY THE GAME & ENJOY EVERY MOMENT

PRIORITIZE WHAT IS IMPORTANT IN YOUR LIFE

"you will never find time for anything. if you want time you must make it"
—charles buxton

THE ONLY THING THAT IS EQUAL IN LIFE IS TIME...

HOW ARE YOU USING IT?

LIST YOUR TOP 3 PRIORITIES & VALUES

LIST 3 ACTIVITIES THAT MAKE YOU SMILE

IT'S OKAY TO SAY "NO" TO PEOPLE & PLACES THAT ARE NOT YOUR HIGHEST PRIORITY

MAKE TIME TO TAKE CARE OF YOURSELF

SELF CARE IS NECESSARY TO BEING THE BEST VERSION OF YOURSELF

"the most powerful relationship you will ever have is the relationship with yourself"
—steve maraboli

LEARN TO LOVE YOURSELF

SITTING WITH THE DARK & LIGHT OF YOUR EXPERIENCES IS PART OF THE JOURNEY

BE COMPASSIONATE & NONJUDGMENTAL

LEARN TO PROCESS YOUR EMOTIONS

CUDDLE ON THE COUCH WITH YOUR FAVORITE BLANKET

TURN OFF YOUR DEVICE EARLY EACH NIGHT

UNWIND YOUR BRAIN FOR BED

DRINK MORE WATER, MOVE YOUR BODY, & GET ADEQUATE SLEEP

ASKING FOR HELP IS A SIGN OF BRAVERY & COURAGE

"it's okay to Not be okay, but it's Not okay to
Not be okay & Not get the help you Need"
—Rob eastman

YOU ARE NOT ALONE & YOU ARE NOT EXPECTED TO KNOW HOW
TO WORK THROUGH EVERYTHING THAT HAPPENS IN YOUR LIFE

FINDING MENTORS WHO CAN HELP YOU THROUGH
CHALLENGES IS THE BEGINNING OF CHANGING YOUR WORLD

REACH OUT TO OTHERS WHO CAN GUIDE YOU ON YOUR JOURNEY

YOU ARE NOT ALONE

YOU ARE LOVED

TAKE THE NEXT RIGHT STEP FOR YOU EVERY SINGLE DAY

"you cannot change your destination overnight, but you can change your direction overnight"
−Jim Rohn

CHANGING DIRECTIONS BEGINS WITH AN IDEA

SHIFT YOUR THINKING & MINDSET

YOU ARE ALWAYS ONE DECISION AWAY FROM
A COMPLETELY DIFFERENT LIFE

YOU MAY NOT SEE THE OUTCOME YET

BUT SMALL STEPS LEAD TO BIG REWARDS

CHANGE ONE THING TODAY THAT YOU CAN CONTROL

SET BOUNDARIES WITH WHAT YOU WILL & WON'T ALLOW INTO YOUR LIFE

"you teach people how to treat you by deciding what you will & won't accept"
—anna taylor

THE WAY OTHERS TREAT YOU CAN BE A REFLECTION OF YOURSELF

PLACE VALUE & WORTH IN WHO YOU ARE

BEGIN POSITIVE SELF TALK AFFIRMATIONS

I VALUE MYSELF AS A PERSON

I DESERVE TO BE HAPPY

I AM STRONG

I CAN STAND UP FOR MYSELF

THE HERO YOU ARE LOOKING FOR IS ALREADY WITHIN

"i think there is a hero in all of us"
—spiderman

BEING A HERO ISN'T JUST THE ENDING OF THE STORY

TRIALS & CHALLENGES APPEAR ALONG THE WAY

YOU ARE THE AUTHOR OF YOUR STORY & YOUR LIFE

GIVE YOURSELF A HIGH-5 IN THE MIRROR EVERY SINGLE MORNING

YOU ARE SEEN

YOU ARE VALUED

YOU ARE LOVED

YOU ARE WORTH IT

PAST CHALLENGES WILL GUIDE YOU WHEN THINGS GET TOUGH

IT'S OKAY NOT TO HAVE ALL THE ANSWERS TO YOUR QUESTIONS

"he who thinks he knows, doesn't know. he who knows that he doesn't know, knows"
—joseph campbell

THE REALITY IS THAT NO ONE REALLY
KNOWS WHAT THEY ARE DOING

THERE IS POWER IN ADMITTING THAT YOU
DON'T KNOW WHAT YOU DON'T KNOW

DOORS WILL OPEN FOR YOU TO LEARN LESSONS

NEW KNOWLEDGE WILL GUIDE NEW ADVENTURES

WORKING THROUGH THE UNKNOWN IS
PART OF THE GROWTH PROCESS

YOUR TIMING IS YOUR TIMING & NOT TO BE DETERMINED BY SOMEONE ELSE'S IDEA FOR YOU

"life's battles don't always go to the stronger or faster man. but sooner or later, the man who wins is the man who thinks he can"
—vince lombardi

YOUR LIFE ISN'T A RACE TO BE WON, IT'S A STORY TO BE LIVED

YOU WILL HAVE BATTLES & STRUGGLES
THAT YOU FACE ALONG THE WAY

BELIEVE IN YOURSELF & KNOW THAT YOU CAN DO THIS

ONE DAY YOU WILL LOOK BACK WITH PRIDE
AT WHAT YOU HAVE OVERCOME

OBSTACLES TEACH YOU HOW TO OVERCOME THE CHALLENGE

"but obstacles don't have to stop you. if you run into a wall, don't turn around & give up. figure out how to climb it, go through it, or work around it"
—michael jordan

THERE IS ALWAYS A SOLUTION IF YOU ARE WILLING TO FIND IT

BE PERSISTENT IN REACHING YOUR GOAL

DON'T LET SOMETHING OR SOMEONE KEEP YOU DOWN

FALL DOWN & GET UP, FALL DOWN & GET UP

KEEP MOVING FORWARD

ROADBLOCKS CAN BE YOUR GREATEST TEACHER, IF YOU LEARN THE LESSON

"everything happens for you, not to you. everything happens at exactly the right moment, neither too soon nor too late. you don't have to like it...it's just easier if you do"
—bryon Katie

YOUR TRIALS CAN BE YOUR BLESSINGS

SHIFT YOUR MINDSET

KNOW THAT YOUR EXPERIENCES ARE VALUABLE TEACHERS

SEE THE OBSTACLES THAT ARISE AS A BENEFIT, LESSON, & ADVANTAGE

IT'S TIME TO TAKE THE NEXT STEP ON YOUR HERO'S JOURNEY

YOUR MIND CAN CREATE THE REALITY YOU WANT

"the more positive you think, the more positivity you attract. a positive person has the ability to light up the mood of everyone around just by entering a room"
—Robert smith

THINK POSITIVELY

YOU WILL ATTRACT THE BEST POSSIBLE OUTCOMES

BE THE LIGHT YOU WANT SOMEONE TO BE FOR YOU

POSITIVE THOUGHTS + POSITIVE ACTIONS = POSITIVE RESULTS

BAD DAYS DON'T NEED TO LAST FOREVER

"don't make a bad day make you feel like you have a bad life"
—UNKNOWN

BAD DAYS ARE GOING TO HAPPEN

THROW YOURSELF A PITY PARTY & MOVE ON

THE LONGER YOU LET THE NEGATIVITY REPLAY

THE LONGER YOU WILL CONTINUE TO HAVE A BAD DAY

YOUR HERO'S STORY BEGINS IN A MOMENT

DECIDE YOU ARE WORTH FIGHTING FOR

YOU ARE WORTH IT

YOUR STORY ISN'T FINISHED

MORNINGS MATTER

"morning is an important time of day because how you spend your morning can often tell you what kind of day you are going to have"
—lemony snicket

CREATE A MORNING ROUTINE THAT WILL
LEAD YOU TO A POSITIVE DAY

MAKE YOUR BED

LISTEN TO AN ENCOURAGING BOOK OR PODCAST

WRITE DOWN 3 THINGS YOU ARE GRATEFUL FOR TODAY

SHOWER

DO YOUR HAIR

BRUSH YOUR TEETH

BE PROUD OF HOW YOU ARE PRESENTING YOURSELF

YOU CANNOT CHANGE
WITHOUT CHANGE

"if you keep on doing what you've always done, you will keep getting what you've always gotten"
—Tony Robbins

MAKE ONE SMALL POSITIVE CHANGE TODAY

DO IT DAILY

CONSISTENCY IS KEY TO GROWTH

READ A SELF-HELP BOOK

LISTEN TO A POWERFUL PODCAST

GET OUT IN NATURE

PRACTICE MINDFULNESS

CREATE POSITIVE PURPOSE FOR WHY YOU ARE ON SOCIAL MEDIA

*"we are what we repeatedly do. excellence
then is not an act, but a habit"
—will durant*

DEVELOP YOUR VOICE & INFLUENCE OTHERS

JOIN IN A CAUSE THAT YOU ARE INTERESTED IN

STOP MINDLESSLY SCROLLING

SET A TIMER FOR HOW LONG YOU CAN
BE ON CERTAIN PLATFORMS

BE INTENTIONAL FOR WHY YOU ARE ONLINE...

IS IT NUMBING & ESCAPING A CURRENT SITUATION?

IS IT FOR ENTERTAINMENT?

IS IT TO FEEL BETTER?

ARE YOU COMPARING YOURSELF TO OTHERS?

CHOOSE TO SEEK OUT POSITIVE CONTENT
THAT IS GOING TO INSPIRE TODAY

BE THE AUTHOR OF YOUR OWN STORY OR SOMEONE ELSE WILL WRITE THE PAGES

"Your life is a story, what's done is done. Where it goes from here is totally up to you. Write your own ending!"
—Jennifer Donnelly

TAKE OWNERSHIP OF YOUR CURRENT REALITY

LOVE YOURSELF THROUGH THIS CHAPTER

MANY CHARACTERS WILL APPEAR IN YOUR STORY

YOU DECIDE WHAT ROLE THEY WILL PLAY

SOMETIMES YOU WILL SPEAK

SOMETIMES YOU WILL PROCESS ON YOUR OWN

SOMETIMES YOU WILL NEED SOMEONE TO
TELL YOU THAT IT'S GOING TO BE OKAY

IT'S GOING TO BE OKAY...YOU ARE ENOUGH

BRAVERY IS DOING SOMETHING, EVEN WHEN YOU KNOW YOU MAY FAIL

"being brave means knowing that when you fail, you don't fail forever"
—lana del rey

BRAVERY LOOKS DIFFERENT FOR EVERY HERO

KNOW THAT YOU WILL BE AFRAID AT TIMES

LEARN THE LESSON FROM YOUR EXPERIENCE

FIND SOMETHING NEW ABOUT YOURSELF

THERE IS NO SUCH THING AS REAL FAILURE

"FAILING FORWARD" IS TRUE BRAVERY

KEEP BEING BRAVE WHILE WRITING YOUR HERO'S STORY

HAVE AN INSPIRING PHOTO, QUOTE, OR AFFIRMATION AS A SCREENSAVER

"i believe one of my strengths is my ability to keep negative thoughts out. i am an optimist"
—john wooden

FOCUS ON WHAT INSPIRES YOU ON THE JOURNEY

I CAN ACHIEVE MY DREAMS

I KNOW PEOPLE LOVE ME

I GIVE MYSELF PERMISSION TO BE ME

I AM PROUD OF MYSELF

I AM ENOUGH

I AM WORTHY

I LOVE MYSELF

I DESERVE HAPPINESS

I BELONG

I AM LOVED

CHOOSE TO BECOME UNIQUELY YOU & KNOW THAT YOU ARE ENOUGH

"i am not what has happened to me. i am what i choose to become"
—carl jung

THERE ARE MANY SITUATIONS YOU DON'T HAVE CONTROL OVER

THOSE CIRCUMSTANCES DON'T DEFINE YOU

CHOOSE TO BECOME WHO YOU WANT TO BE

IT WILL TAKE TIME TO SHIFT YOUR MINDSET

IT IS POSSIBLE TO CHANGE YOUR FUTURE

YOUR PAST DOES NOT HAVE TO BE YOUR FUTURE

CHANGE STARTS WITH YOU

IT'S YOUR MOMENT

BE YOURSELF

"find what makes your heart sing & create your own music"
—mac anderson

DO WHAT YOU LOVE

EVEN IF YOU ARE THE ONLY ONE WHO LOVES IT

FIND SOMETHING THAT MAKES YOUR HEART SING

DECIDE TODAY THAT YOU DETERMINE WHAT'S "COOL" FOR YOU

YOUR GIFTS CAN INSPIRE THE WORLD

FIND FRIENDS THAT YOU BELONG WITH, NOT ONES YOU HAVE TO CHANGE FOR

"why fit in when you were born to stand out?"
—dr. seuss

YOU DO NOT NEED TO CHANGE YOURSELF
TO MAKE SOMEONE ELSE HAPPY

STOP PRETENDING TO BE SOMEONE ELSE
TO BE LIKED OR "ACCEPTED"

THOSE WHO BELONG IN YOUR LIFE

WILL LOVE YOU

WILL ACCEPT YOU

WILL EMBRACE ALL YOUR BEAUTIFUL FLAWS

IT'S OKAY TO NOT BE FRIENDS WITH EVERYONE

IT'S OKAY TO NOT HAVE MANY FRIENDS

LOVE YOURSELF FIRST

THOSE WHO BELONG IN YOUR LIFE WILL STAY

HAPPINESS CAN EXIST EVEN WHEN YOU ARE STRUGGLING

"it does Not do to dwell on dreams & forget to live, Remember tha-"
—albus dumbledore

CHOOSE TO KEEP MOVING FORWARD

NO MATTER THE LOSS, GRIEF, HEARTACHE,
OR TRAUMA THAT HAS TAKEN PLACE

CHOOSE HAPPINESS TODAY

IT DOESN'T MEAN YOU DON'T HAVE SCARS FROM YOUR PAST

IT MEANS THAT YOU ARE COPING

YOU ARE CHOOSING JOY IN THE JOURNEY

HAPPINESS IS CREATED IN EACH NEW MOMENT

"happiness cannot be traveled to, owned, earned, worn, or consumed. happiness is the spiritual experience of living every minute with love, grace, & gratitude"
—denis waitley

DO SOMETHING FUN EVERY SINGLE DAY

SMILE

LAUGH

ENJOY YOUR LIFE

ACTIONS CREATE HAPPINESS

HAVE COURAGE TO DO THINGS THAT MAKE YOU GRATEFUL

EVERY MOMENT IS A MOMENT TO CELEBRATE

GRATITUDE IS THE QUICKEST WAY TO CHANGE YOUR ATTITUDE

"there's nothing more important than attitude, & it's your choice"
—mike KRZyzewski

ATTITUDE IS ONE OF THE ONLY THINGS YOU
HAVE CONTROL OVER IN YOUR LIFE

MAKE A GRATITUDE LIST TODAY

MAKE THE CHOICE TO BE POSITIVE

LOOK FOR CREATIVE WAYS TO SOLVE DIFFICULT SITUATIONS

CHOOSE A POSITIVE WORD FOR YOUR ATTITUDE EACH DAY...

BE JOYFUL

BE OPTIMISTIC

BE HOPEFUL

BE ENCOURAGED

THIS MOMENT COULD BE THE MOMENT THAT CHANGES YOUR LIFE FOREVER

"enjoy the little things, for one day you may look back & realize they were the big things"
—Robert Brault

CONSCIOUSLY CREATE DAILY GRATITUDE FOR THE SMALL THINGS

SHOW APPRECIATION TO IMPROVE RELATIONSHIPS

CONNECTIONS OPEN DOORS FOR MORE OPPORTUNITIES

BE GRATEFUL & CREATE HOPE FOR THE FUTURE

INSPIRE YOURSELF & OTHERS

BRING MORE POSITIVE MOMENTS INTO YOUR LIFE

BE HERE IN THE NOW, KNOWING THAT THERE IS A LESSON YOU ARE GOING TO LEARN

"i may not have gone where i intended to go, but i think i have ended up where i needed to be"
—douglas adams

YOU WILL NOT ALWAYS GET WHERE YOU WANTED TO GO

THERE ARE CIRCUMSTANCES THAT CHANGE THE DIRECTION

TRUST THAT YOU ARE WHERE YOU NEED TO BE

RIGHT NOW...FOR THE RIGHT REASON

LEARN, GROW, BECOME

THE BEST VERSION OF YOURSELF IN THE
PLACE YOU ARE IN RIGHT NOW

BE PROUD OF YOUR MISTAKES BECAUSE THEY TRANSFORM YOU INTO A BETTER VERSION OF YOURSELF

*"if not mistake you have made, losing you are.
a different game you should play"*
—yoda

MAKING MISTAKES MEANS THAT YOU ARE TRYING NEW THINGS

MISTAKES ARE TEACHERS

YOU CANNOT EXPECT TO BEGIN EVERY NEW
ADVENTURE KNOWING THE WAY

YOU MUST MAKE MISTAKES, CORRECT THE COURSE, & TRY AGAIN

EXPLORE BEYOND YOUR COMFORT ZONE

BECOMING WHO YOU ARE MEANT TO BE REQUIRES CHANGE

DARE TO FAIL AT SOMETHING

HOPE LIGHTS PURPOSE WITHIN US & AROUND US

"learn from yesterday, live for today, hope for tomorrow"
—albert einstein

HOPE GIVES YOU BELIEF

TRUST THAT THE IMPOSSIBLE IS POSSIBLE

THE POWER IS WITHIN YOU TO CHOOSE HOPE

THE DIRECTION YOU GO AFTER FACING A CHALLENGE IS UP TO YOU

EMPOWER YOURSELF TO BELIEVE THAT YOU
CAN DO THINGS THAT ARE HARD & SCARY

BELIEVE IN SOMETHING BIGGER THAN YOURSELF

YOU ARE BECOMING STRONGER AS YOU OVERCOME TRIALS

YOU ARE WORTH BELIEVING IN

A HERO ACCEPTS THE CALL WITHOUT KNOWING ALL THE ANSWERS

"a hero is someone who, in spite of weakness, doubt or not always knowing the answers, goes ahead & overcomes anyway"
—christopher reeve (superman)

ALONG THE WAY, YOU BECOME WHO YOU ARE MEANT TO BE

YOU ARE SUPPOSED TO HAVE FLAWS

YOU WILL NOT HAVE IT ALL FIGURED OUT
BEFORE YOU START YOUR ADVENTURE

YOU WILL FIND THE ANSWERS YOU SEEK
ARE ALREADY WITHIN YOU

TAKE THIS STEP

THEN TAKE THE NEXT ONE

IF YOU WAIT FOR THE PERFECT MOMENT, YOU WILL NEVER GET THE CHANCE

"some people spend their entire lives waiting for the
time to be right to make an improvement"
—james clear

THERE WILL NEVER BE THE "RIGHT" TIME FOR EVERYTHING

TAKE A STEP TODAY

BEGIN SOMETHING YOU HAVE WANTED TO START

TAKE INSPIRED & IMPERFECT ACTION TOWARDS A GOAL

BE CONFIDENT & COURAGEOUS IN YOUR ACTION

TRUST YOUR INTUITION

KNOW THAT YOU WILL BE GUIDED ALONG THE WAY

WHEN YOU DOUBT YOURSELF, REMEMBER THAT THERE IS SOMEONE WHO IS READY TO HELP YOU FIND THE LIGHT

"when the hero is ready, the mentor appears"
—Will Craig

YOU ARE NOT EXPECTED TO JOURNEY
THROUGH THIS LIFE ON YOUR OWN

FIND SOMEONE YOU CAN TRUST

REMEMBER THAT THIS PERSON MAY NOT BE THE
YODA FIGURE YOU IMAGINED IN YOUR MIND

FIND SOMEONE WHO HAS YOUR BEST INTEREST AT HEART

FIND SOMEONE WHO WILL SUPPORT YOU THROUGH THE UNKNOWN

BELIEVE IN YOUR ABILITIES TO BECOME
WHO YOU ARE MEANT TO BE

BE OPEN TO POSSIBILITIES THAT WEREN'T PLANNED BECAUSE THEY MIGHT BE YOUR GREATEST GIFT

"we must be willing to let go of the life we planned
so as to have the life that is waiting for us"
—joseph campbell

THE JOURNEY ISN'T MADE WITH AN EXACT "TO-DO" LIST

YOU WILL HAVE PLANS & THEN PLANS CHANGE

ADJUST & PIVOT

KNOW THAT THE PATHS YOU TRAVEL MAY NOT BE THE SAME AS YOU IMAGINED IN YOUR MIND

WHEN YOU TRUST YOURSELF, OTHERS WILL TRUST YOU TOO

"follow your inner heart & the world moves in & helps"
—joseph campbell

YOUR INTUITION WILL GUIDE YOU THROUGH YOUR HERO'S JOURNEY

LISTEN TO THE VOICE THAT WHISPERS
INSIDE YOU & CREATES BUTTERFLIES

THIS IS THE VOICE OF YOUR HEART ALIGNING YOU WITH PURPOSE

THE BUTTERFLY EFFECT TRULY MEANS
THAT YOU CAN CHANGE THE WORLD

LISTEN

ACT

SPREAD YOUR WINGS & FLY

YOU ARE THE ONLY YOU & THAT IS ONE INCREDIBLE CREATION

"the privilege of a lifetime is being who you are"
-joseph campbell

CELEBRATE THE FREEDOM OF BEING THE
ONLY YOU IN THE UNIVERSE

YOU WERE BORN WITH INFINITE WORTH

YOU DON'T HAVE TO PROVE ANYTHING TO ANYONE

EMBRACE & LOVE THE BEAUTIFUL MESS THAT EXISTS WITHIN YOU

ACKNOWLEDGE THAT YOU ARE EXPERIENCING A
NEW LIFE & NEW DAY WITH EACH SUNRISE

YOU MUST DARE TO TAKE THE FIRST STEP & LEAP OF FAITH

"that step, the heroic first step of the journey, is out of or over the edge of your boundaries, & it often must be taken before you know that you will be supported"
—joseph campbell

TO GROW YOURSELF, YOU MUST PUSH BEYOND
THE BOUNDARIES OF YOUR COMFORT ZONE

TAKE A LEAP OF FAITH

THE NET WILL APPEAR

THOSE WHO ARE PART OF YOUR JOURNEY,
WILL APPEAR ALONG THE WAY

CHOICES YOU MAKE TODAY WILL CREATE YOUR REALITY OF TOMORROW

"i attribute my success to this: i never gave or took any excuse"
—florence nightingale

BLAMING OTHERS WILL NEVER GET YOU ANYWHERE

EXCUSES WILL KEEP YOU FROM REACHING YOUR POTENTIAL

LET GO OF COMPLAINING

START DOING

MAKE CHOICES THAT ALIGN

WITH WHO YOU WANT TO BE

NOW & IN THE FUTURE

CHOOSE YOUR PATH & BECOME THE HERO YOU ARE MEANT TO BE

"heroes are made by the paths they choose,
not the power they are graced with"
—brodi ashton

YOU ARE NOT CALLED ON A HERO'S ADVENTURE
EQUIPPED WITH ALL THAT YOU NEED

TOOLS & KNOWLEDGE ARE EARNED ALONG THE PATH

SMALL CHOICES CREATE BIG RESULTS

OVERCOME STRUGGLE & DEFEAT

IGNITE THE POWER WITHIN YOU TO RISE

GO FORWARD WITH STRENGTH

KNOW THAT YOU WILL LEARN & SUCCEED ONE STEP AT A TIME

THE WORK YOU DO THAT OTHERS NEVER SEE IS WHERE THE SEEDS OF HOPE & CHANGE ARE PLANTED

"change is your friend not your foe; change is a brilliant opportunity to grow"
—simon t. bailey

NEW PERSPECTIVE ARISES WITH CHANGE

EMBRACE CHANGE AS A LEARNING OPPORTUNITY

CHANGE TEACHES YOU TO BE RESILIENT

CHANGE TEACHES YOU TO BE ADAPTABLE

CHANGE TEACHES YOU TO BE OPEN-MINDED

SELF DISCOVERY LEADS TO SELF-CONFIDENCE

AGAIN & AGAIN YOU WILL FIGHT THE SAME CHALLENGE UNTIL YOU RISE, FACE IT, & OVERCOME IT

"oh yes, the past can hurt. but the way i see it,
you can either RUN from it, or learn from it"
—Rafiki

TURN PAST SITUATIONS INTO OPPORTUNITIES TO STRENGTHEN YOUR CHARACTER

FACE IT

UNDERSTAND IT

NEW WISDOM CREATES COURAGE & CONFIDENCE

MAKE A CHANGE

DISCOVER A GROWTH MINDSET

THE ROAD TO DISCOVER THE HERO WITHIN WILL HAVE LOTS OF CHALLENGES ALONG THE WAY

"sometimes the right path is not the easiest one"
—grandmother willow

STAY TRUE TO YOUR INTEGRITY, MORALS, & ETHICS

LET THEM BE YOUR GUIDE AS YOU FACE ADVERSITY

AT TIMES YOU MAY FORGET THE STRENGTH WITHIN

COME BACK TO YOUR BELIEFS

THEY WILL GUIDE YOU ALONG THE PATH OF HOPE

YOU HAVE WHAT IT TAKES TO MAKE THE RIGHT CHOICE

YOUR STORY ISN'T FINISHED...
IT'S JUST BEGINNING

"sometimes the hardest battle is against yourself.
but believe in yourself & you can win"
—UNKNOWN

LIVE THE LIFE YOU WERE DESTINED TO FOLLOW

LET GO OF THE IDEAS THAT ARE KEEPING YOU DOWN

BE

DO

ACT

LOOK

DISCOVER THE INCREDIBLE STRENGTH WITHIN

YOU ARE TALENTED

STAY DETERMINED TO SHINE

IT'S TIME TO BELIEVE IN YOU

IT IS NOT WHAT YOU ARE GIVEN IN LIFE, IT'S WHAT YOU CHOOSE TO DO WITH WHO YOU ARE

"it is not our abilities that show us what
we truly are...it is our choices"
—albus dumbledore

YOU HAVE THE POWER TO CREATE

CHOOSE YOUR DESTINY

IT DOESN'T MATTER WHAT ABILITIES YOU WERE BORN WITH

IT MATTERS WHAT YOU CHOOSE TO DO WITH THEM

YOUR THOUGHTS & ACTIONS WILL INFLUENCE
HOW YOU FEEL ABOUT YOURSELF

CHOOSE ACTIONS THAT WILL CREATE POSITIVE OUTCOMES

LOOK INSIDE & KNOW THAT YOU ARE THE MIRACLE & THE HERO

"the miracle is not some magic that you've got. the miracle is you, not some gift, just you. the miracle is you, all of you...all of you"
—encanto

PLACE YOUR HAND ON YOUR HEART...

CLOSE YOUR EYES

LISTEN TO THE SOUND

BREATHE IN & OUT (REPEAT 3X))

CREATE YOUR OWN BEAUTIFUL & UNEXPECTED EXPERIENCES

YOU ARE THE GIFT

IT IS YOUR TURN TO SHINE

START OWNING YOUR VOICE

TRUST THAT YOU BELONG

CHOOSE TO BE THE STAR PLAYER IN YOUR STORY

"Never let the fear of striking out keep
you from playing the game"
—babe Ruth

YOU WILL STRIKE OUT MANY TIMES ON THIS JOURNEY

DON'T LET THOSE STRIKEOUTS KEEP YOU
FROM GETTING BACK UP AGAIN

YOU DECIDE

ARE GOING TO PLAY THE GAME OR SIT ON THE SIDELINES

NEVER LET YOUR FEAR KEEP YOU FROM
PLAYING IN YOUR GAME OF LIFE

LET'S PLAY

RISE & RISE AGAIN, NO MATTER HOW MANY TIMES YOU FALL DOWN

"you will face many defeats in life, but
Never let yourself be defeated"
—maya angelou

GET UP EACH TIME YOU FALL DOWN

THERE WILL BE PEOPLE WHO DON'T BELIEVE YOU CAN DO IT

THOSE ARE NOT THE PEOPLE WHO BELONG WITH YOU

BELIEVE IN YOURSELF

BELIEVE IN THE PROCESS

BELIEVE THAT NO MATTER WHAT HAPPENS

YOU CAN RISE ABOVE ANY DEFEAT THAT COMES YOUR WAY

YOU ARE CAPABLE

YOU ARE WORTHY

BE THE HERO OF YOUR OWN STORY

MAKE YOUR OWN PATH FULL OF EXCITING ADVENTURES & BEAUTY

"do not go where the path may lead, go instead
where there's no path & leave a trail"
—Ralph Waldo Emerson

BE COURAGEOUS IN CREATING A PATH OF HAPPINESS

ENJOY FRIENDSHIPS & LEARNING FROM MISTAKES

GROW INTO THE PERSON YOU ARE MEANT TO BE

CHANGE THE WORLD

BEAUTIFUL ADVENTURES ARE TO BE LIVED & EXPERIENCED BY YOU

MAKE YOUR OWN TRAIL FOR OTHERS TO FOLLOW

NO MATTER THE PAST & PRESENT, YOU ARE THE CREATOR OF YOUR FUTURE

"go confidently in the direction of your dreams!
live the life you've imagined"
—henry david thoreau

DREAM

CREATE

IMAGINE

BELIEVE

YOU HAVE THE ABILITY TO DESIGN THE LIFE YOU WANT

YOU ARE THE BUILDER OF YOUR DREAMS

DREAM BIG & DREAM OFTEN

TAKE ACTION IN THE DIRECTION OF YOUR DREAMS

ACHIEVE YOUR DESTINY

IT'S TIME TO BE THE HERO OF YOUR OWN STORY

"you are the hero of your own story"
—joseph campbell

YOU WILL HAVE MANY DIFFERENT ADVENTURES

YOU ARE DESTINED FOR GREATNESS

MENTORS ARE WILLING TO HELP YOU REACH YOUR POTENTIAL

REMEMBER YOU WILL HAVE FRIENDS & FOES ALONG THE WAY

TRUST YOUR INTUITION IN KNOWING
WHO BELONGS IN YOUR STORY

LESSONS LEARNED FROM PREVIOUS TRIALS
WILL BE A CONSTANT GUIDE

YOU HAVE THE POWER WITHIN YOU TO BE
THE HERO YOU ARE MEANT TO BE

IT'S TIME

HERO

ABOUT THE AUTHOR

I am a dynamic educator who has been teaching teens in the classroom and coaching students to become the hero of their own stories for 14+ years. I have a Master's Degree in Educational Leadership, a Bachelor's Degree in Psychology and English, and I am a qualified youth mentor and resiliency coach.

In addition, I am nationally certified in QPR Suicide Prevention, run a Hope Squad course, and collaborate with youth mentors and prevention programs throughout my community.

I believe mindset plays a huge role in the level of success, love, and abundance you will achieve in life. The decisions you make today will create the pathway to your future.

Passion for personal growth and action has profoundly impacted my success, career, family, finances, and relationships. I am so excited to become your teacher & coach on this journey!

It's time to show you how you can become the hero of your own story!

Your success story begins now!

Xo, Elysia Butler

Website–www.thehopehero.com
Mentorship Options–Self Study, Group Coaching, and Individual Programs
Instagram–@risewithelysia @thehopehero
Facebook–Elysia Butler
TikTok–@iamahopehero
Email–risewithelysia@gmail.com

REVIEWS

"The book was really effective and definitely helped me in my everyday life. It gave some really good tips and tricks for a variety of different things. There's something in the book for so many issues that teens struggle with. Not only does it help teens, it helps their parents. I shared some of the information with my mom and she also really enjoyed it. The format of the book was amazing." (Tatum, age 13)

"This book really helps me to know that it's okay to struggle. Everybody is human, and this helps to remind us that we can make mistakes, and that's okay. This really helps me have inner peace and remember to center myself. The book was formatted so well, and it's great for anyone who needs a little self-esteem boost!" (Reese, 15)

"Become the Hero of Your Own Story" is very influential to me. As a teenager it touched my heart. I feel like I can relate to this book and the tips given. The tips are organized and explained with a quote. It is well laid out and easy to read." (Preston, 15)

"As a parent of teens, *Become the Hero of Your Own Story*, has helped me start important conversations with my kids. Together we have been guided in building strong personal and emotional foundations. Every week we have learned valuable tools in optimism and resilience. Every teen, parent, and adult can benefit from what this book has to offer." (Tara, 36, Mom of 4)

This book was amazing! As a parent of a teen, it helped me connect with my daughter and provide us with uplifting thoughts and messages to discuss. It helped her to improve her mental health and gain more confidence in herself. Also, it opened up the door for us to discuss in-depth issues teens face today. I really liked this book. It helped me learn more about who I am becoming, discover myself, and believe in myself. I will definitely recommend it to my friends. (Melissa, 39, Mom of 3)